DANCE JEANS & POEMS

Silvia Prado dos Anjos
@poeta008

CONTENTS

1. FOREWORDS 5

2. TIME-SPACE-BODY-IMAGE-PRODUCT.... 14

   2.1 TIME-SPACE... 23

   2.2 ... > < ... SELF-RE-CREATION BODY-IMAGE-PRODUCT.. 36

3. AUTHOR'S NOTE (Poetry Bonus).......... 45

   all digital arts by
   Silvia Prado dos Anjos
4. AKA Nylaia @poeta008

A POETICAL

REVOLUTIONARY ESSAY

ON GLIMPSES OF

THE ART OF DANCING

IN REGARD

TO

JEANS PANTS

MARKETING STRATEGIES

AND POETRY BONUS

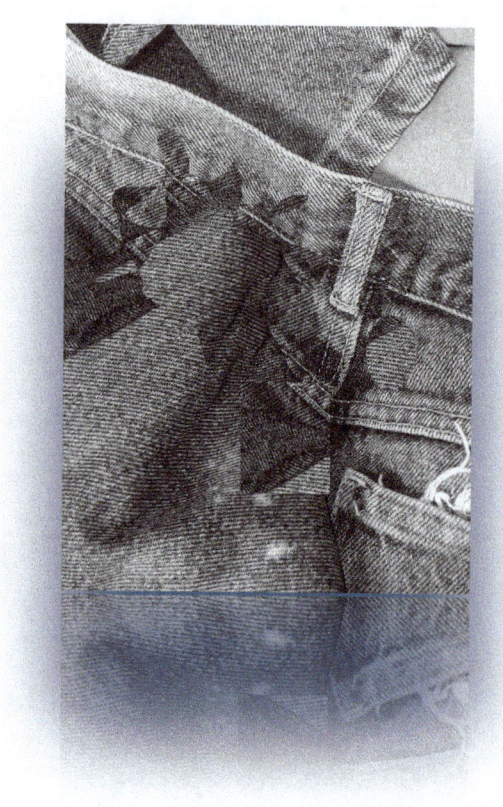

dedicated to Sílvia Sangirardi

I. <u>FOREWORDS</u>

...bring me thy soul...

...I shall take thee to a flow

...bring me to thy flow

...I shall make thee an oar

...bring me thy oar

...I shall make thee ...

The moment now requires

an investment in empowering the

creative aspects of human beings –

at once, the one who wishes –

desire for transformation, and the

one who transforms as well as get

being transformed

by the surrounding environment –

to be the one to conduct a

creative subtle revolution.

At the turning of the twentieth

first century

I was about to apply for a graduation studies program in the United States of America.

By the beginning of the month of June, 2001 I got the news that my beloved father was in comma at the hospital in Brazil.

He had had a stroke.

Mario Negreiros dos Anjos, my dad was born in the middle of the Amazon Forest at the city called Maués, in Amazon state, where Guaraná plant fruits (Paullinia cupana) were abounding.

He moved to the city of Niterói in Rio de Janeiro state to pursue his medical studies

at Fluminense Federal University – UFF; and a few years later.

There he became monitor at the medical program.

He, then got married to Cláudia Maris who was one of his tutoring students at the medical college.

Dad, soon became a well known and dedicated researcher Endocrinology Doctor in Niterói, Brazil having published books on Diabetes and Obesity.

Thus, back to me, my 2001 plans for engaging in studies at the US

immediately lost importance when I understood it was time for me to be near both dad and mom.

I felt the call to return home to be at my dad's side while providing emotional support to my mother as well as brothers, nephews, cousins, aunties, all our family, friends, and aggregates.

Three years later, meanwhile the general health of my dad was quickly turning to a hard-to-recover condition, or to an understanding of the limits one can bear a reasonable living in sanity
I reached an inner openness

to embrace the insight of a call for myself on-demanding for survival.

Thus I decided to apply for a just launched program on Global Marketing certification studies, in Niterói where we live with the idea to research on luxury brands of Jeans marketing strategies.

That was the self-empowering

turning point I definitely needed in
order to reconnect myself to myself;
to be assure of the importance of
keeping up with my vitality,
my braveness, my strength in

facing difficulties the way I learned
for many years by being the leader of
the Brazilian National

Artistic Gymnastics team during the
decade of the seventies (from 1973,
my first Brazilian National

Students Championship – JEBs, till
the closing of my athletic career in
1980 at the South-American
Gymnastics Championship in

Santiago, Chile.

There I conquered the gold medal on the Uneven-Parallel-Bars routine, always my specialty.

I also accomplished to be a finalist at the First American Cup in 1976 at the Madison Square Garden when the Romanian Nadia Comaneci scored the perfect ten for the first time in Gymnastics history.

That being said, let me return to the central idea of this revolutionary essay on glimpses of the Art of Dancing in regarding to a poetical approach of Jeans pants marketing strategies.

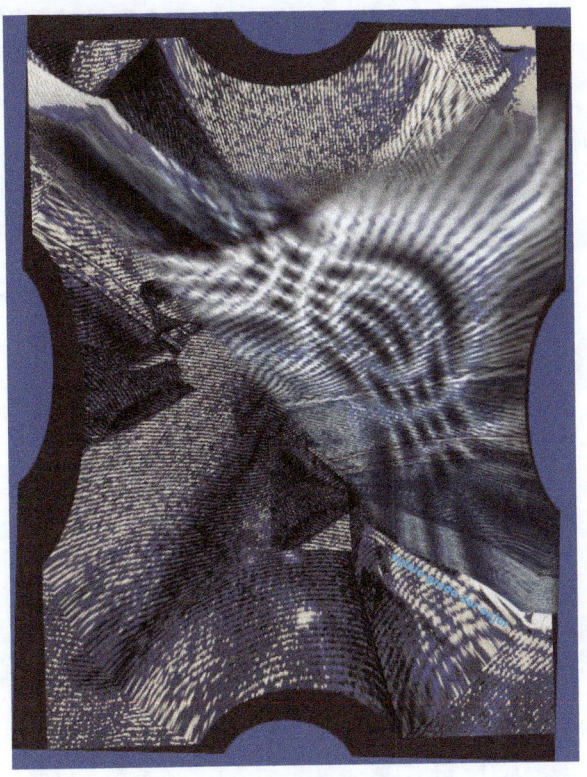

Virtual Design Composition on Jeans Pants
photography & design by Silvia Prado dos Anjos
(@poeta008 nylaia prado dos anjos)

2. TIME – SPACE – BODY – IMAGE – PRODUCT

An ever-changing world demands a reflective attitude in the face of questions about system of values, beliefs and power leaderships in various sectors of the current hard-to-predict consumerism market place.

All-inclusive

        mechanisms

        imprison

creators

        within

            their creations.

The product, jeans pants have an interesting peculiar characteristic along the facts of its

historical evolution.

In despite of the fact that the pants were first designed to dress gold miner workers,

they broke up all general established dressing standard-codes by indeed promoting a revolution.

Jeans pants are a

representative expression of

an uniform and a luxury.

They shall keep, most probably an eternal living in the market place as a unique product that can be universal and selective.

This process of strategically transforming of a mass-consumption product into a personal luxury, in fact brings forth another question of what kind of value could be added to a product that could also preserve its originality?

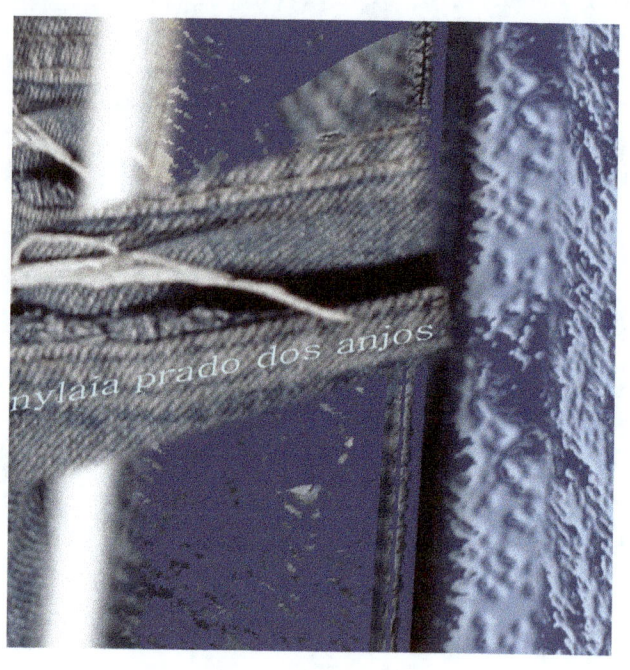

Virtual Design Composition on Jeans Pants
photography & design by Silvia Prado dos Anjos
(@poeta008 nylaia prado dos anjos)

The art of dancing reveals

the dancing body as a

product of a subtle

harmonisation of conflicts –

the muscular tension needed to produce movements.

The body moves through
contradictions when
it turns

    images into thoughts;
      into shapes;
      into feelings;
 into a freely expression of one'self

into a movement

of

dance

that is consumed

in the very moment

of its liberation.

Images move...

...into ideas...feelings...

...motions...

What is the matter

    that weaves

    images into motion?

    In order to investigate the matter
suggested by the question above,

I will briefly sketch a parallel

    between some

    facts of the jeans' history
at the consumer's market place and
some aspects of the origins of dance
in a few different cultures

I've experienced
myself for being also dancer,
performer and storyteller

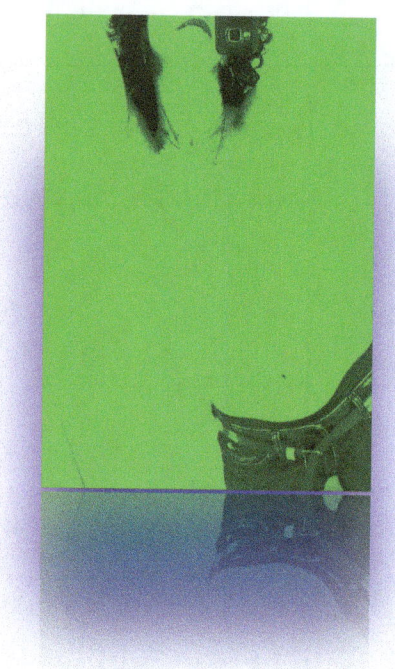

2.1. <u>TIME – SPACE</u>

The German born Mr. Oscar Levi Strauss arrived in the United States of America during the 19th century.

He had the idea of improving the design and manufacturing of hard-workers pants using denim – a thick durable cotton similar fabric to the material that was used to the manufacturing of sailors' uniforms in Gênes –

the French word for the city of Genova, or Genoa in Italy.

Mr. Strauss and his partner Mr. Jacob Davis worked on the development of the initial garment design introducing copper rivets to reinforce areas such as the pockets which were designed to support the usage stress of the pants for long periods of wearing, as well as the carriage of working tools.

They also developed a novelty to the general clothing market by making available close-fitting pants on denim indigo blue color.

They received the patent for their garment's design in 1873.

Those pants turned to being the ever living Blue Jeans.

A product that,
even tough
receiving updates,
transformation in subtleness,
in values' addition and details
got its originality
all well preserved.

In 1950, the pants got zippers and were allied to the revolutionary hip movements of Elvis Presley; to the sensuality of movie stars.

During the sixties the Jeans became 'hippie'.

The denim indigo blue is a fabric that changes in color and texture with use, exposure to light and washings.

Industrial-washed jeans were available in the consumer market, in 1974.

Since then, the Jeans pants as a product they keep on multiplying valuable functions:

Jeans form – they are a basic ready-to-wear garment;

Jeans inform – they are representatives of communication codes;

Jeans transform – they are a vehicle for seduction embodiment.

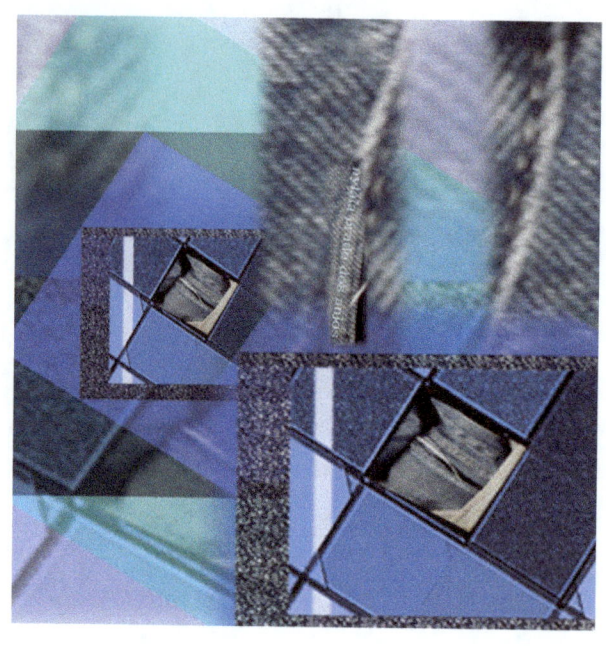

Virtual Design Composition on Jeans Pants
photography & design by Silvia Prado dos Anjos
(nylaia prado dos anjos)

Through time,
the body has served as an instrument for perpetuating through dance human impressions about universal cycles; beauty, harmony,
the force of nature, facts, symbols and myths as well as to
linking diverse people and cultures; even to manifesting a communion amongst obscure,
sacred or profane dimensions.

The Japanese culture connects the origins of dance with the seasons.

Nature's metamorphosis is represented in the Dance of the Butterfly.

Ancient Chinese dances utilised garments with extra-long sleeves.

This fact could represent an expression of transcendence of body limits.

The European Renaissance Classical Dance, also known as Court Dance was derived from movements of the folk dances of the region.

The image of the Dance of Shiva in the Hindu mythology conveys the complexity of perpetual motion;

the process of creation,

maintenance and

destruction/transformation
of universal cycles.

The name Bharata – mythical Hindu creator of the performing arts – is an acronym formed by the three first syllables of the three vital aspects of the
Indian performing arts:

Bhavam –
expression of emotion;

Ragam –melody;

Talam – rhythm.

The gods dance.

The humans dance to
telling their stories.

According to the native Brazilians, body, music and dance are unboundedly inscribed in the magical ritualistic life of the tribe.

They are one unique organism that by being broken apart would lose its sense of unity:

Dance is song;

Dance is chant;

Dance is body;

Dance is in the song of the body.

By analogy,

the body in dancing movement is comprehended as in a rhythmic unity of a musical compass –
the value of the note;

yet it is at once, also a rhythmic absolute value – the compass;
in which the external movement (pressure on a string) and
the intrinsic movement (vibration of the string) merge into a
third movement: that is the sound –
the dancing body.

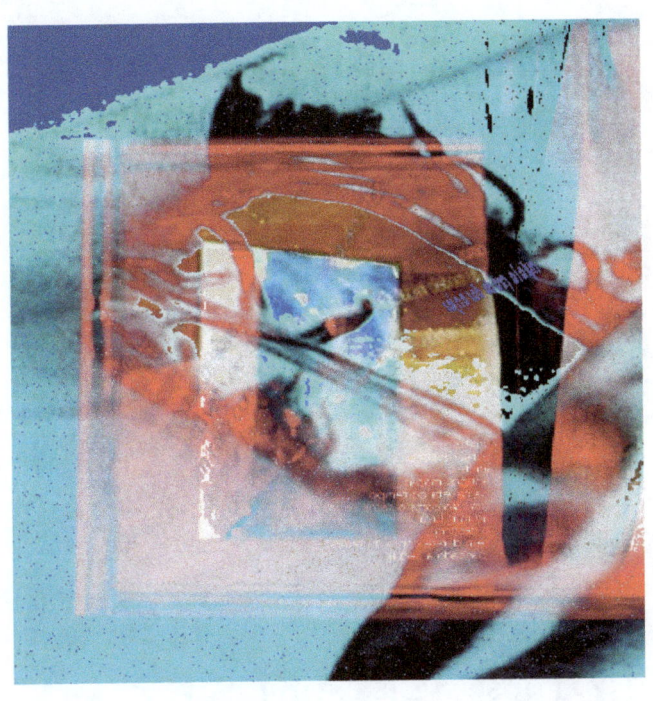

Virtual Design Composition on Jeans Pants
photography by Silvia Prado dos Anjos
(nylaia prado dos anjos)

2.2. ... >   < ... <u>SELF-RE-CREATION</u>
<u>BODY – IMAGE – PRODUCT</u>

Dance, poetically reveals the body anew to the body
in the form of movement signs from an intimate body language.

Those signs extinguish themselves at the moment of its own creation when
they become the representation of a unique dance expression.

The body renews its cells at each and every moment in the metabolic continuum motto.

This means that the dancing body structures self-consuming signs that materialize themselves in a poetical self continuum re-creation of the body itself by each moment of experiencing a movement of dance.

The Jeans' marketing strategies could also be perceived like a self-consuming structure in a parallel point of view to the Art of Dancing.

The moment the consumer acquires a product it opens a lacuna

that will be filled by
the use of the product.

    Thereby the act of consuming Jeans could indicate that
the value given by consumers to the product returns to themselves
as a self-expression.

    The garment, then dresses its consumer

    with self-recognition.

Moreover, it becomes the missing-link for the consumer to being, literally recognised in entering into an unbounded universe
of perfection, in quality, originality, versatility and authenticity promoted by Jeans marketing strategies.

The consumer buys a product that is far beyond its materiality.

What is bought is the concept of this new-born self-image that becomes a reality
in the usage of the product.

This promotes a direct link between the concrete quality of the garment, its fabric, finishing, etc... and its expression of extraordinary being, its authenticity, originality.

The consumers paradoxically incorporate both material and intrinsic values of the Jeans in an attitude towards self-appraising.

Thus, the consuming of Jeans seems to reflect a range of values that privileges ephemeral poetical

creative values over

hard materialistic established ones, however those values in fact become of a way, a guidance to a unique extraordinary self-image resetting experience.

Image

merges into body

Body-image

merges into product

Body-image-product
represents the experience

of one' self-re-creation.

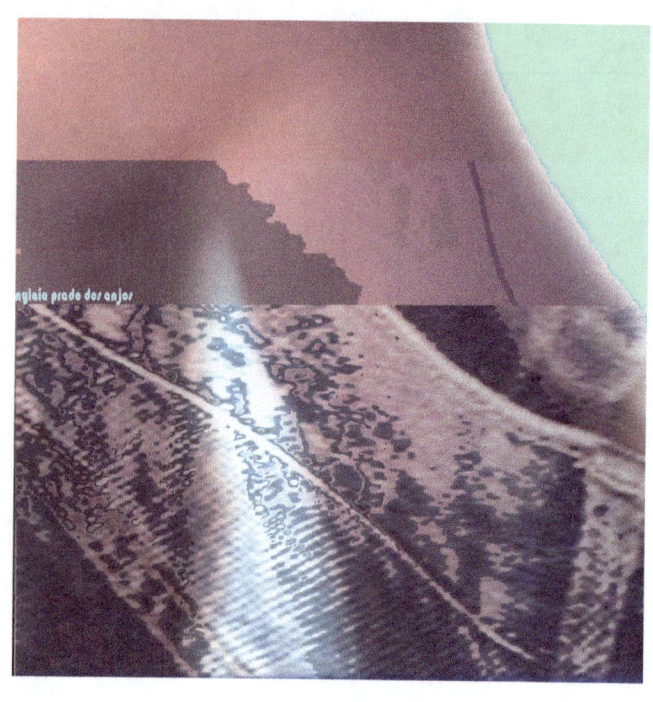

Virtual Design Composition on Jeans Pants

photography by Silvia Prado dos Anjos

(nylaia prado dos anjos)

Finally to conclude I shall bring forth this freely translation of a poem by one of my very best friends
Mrs. Sílvia Sangirardi (1946-1999) a fabulous one-of-a-kind extraordinary human being besides a well-know Brazilian costume designer, actress , astrologist, marvellous witch and writer:

                        panning

                            stars for

               gold

              is

                     the garment'

                   saying

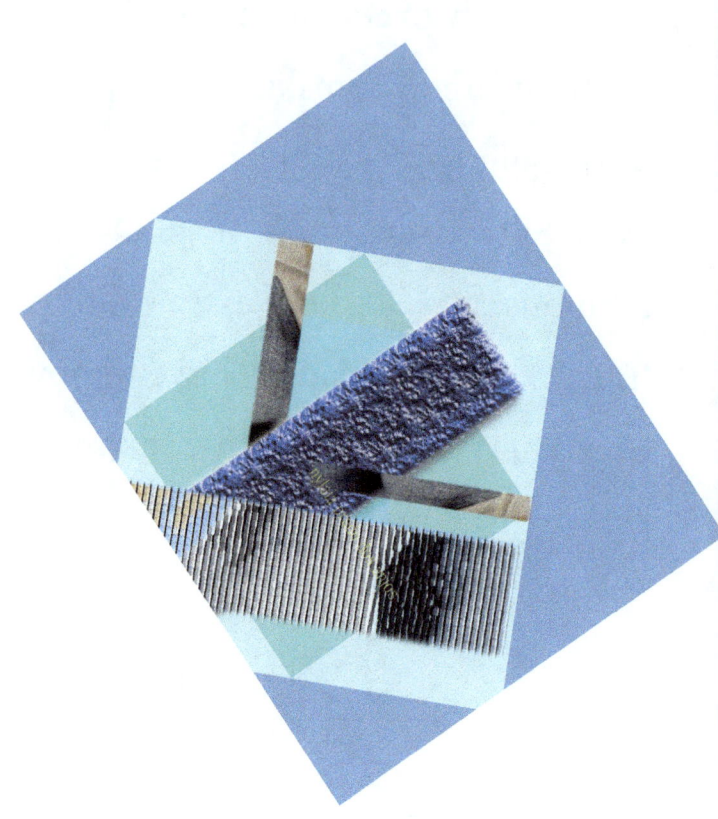

Virtual Design Composition on Jeans Pants
photography by Silvia Prado dos Anjos
(nylaia prado dos anjos)

Author's notes

The decision to publish these ideas happened to me at a moment I needed to endure what I believe shall be one of the hardest suffering in my life, that was to witness the grieving for the loss of beloved ones.

This moment urges a call for attentive regards to the eternal essential individual questions that I understand by :

WHO AM I?

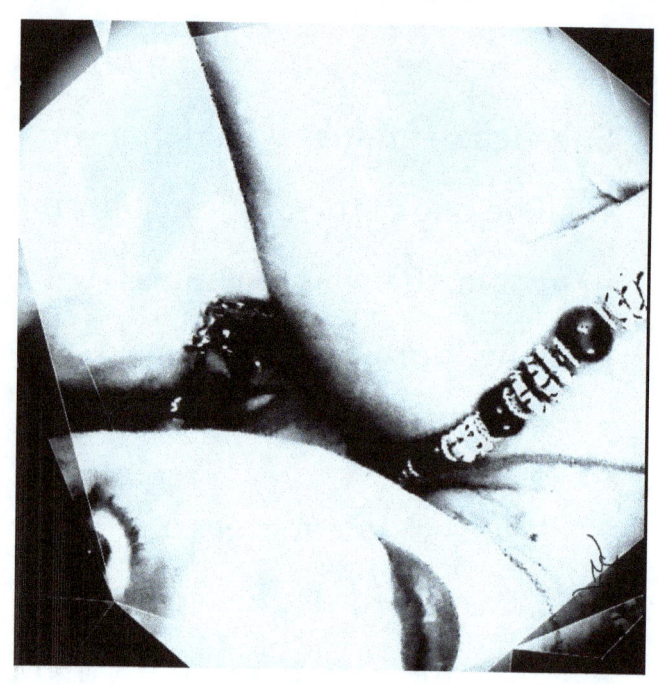

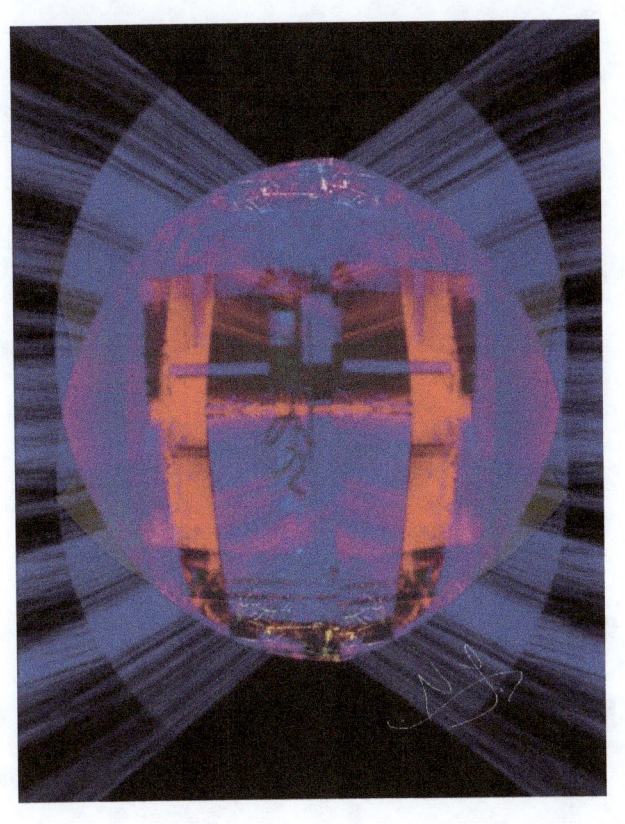

WHAT AM I HERE FOR?

DO I MAKE SENSE?

... >   < ...

WHAT FEELS THE NIGHT

TOUCHING THE MOON

    WHAT FEELS THE MOON

    TOUCHING THE WIND

WHAT FEELS THE WIND

TOUCHING THE LEAVES

      WHAT FEELS THE LEAVES

      TOUCHING SOME BLUES

WHAT FEELS THE BLUES

TOUCHING THE SKIN

      WHAT FEELS THE SKIN

      TOUCHING THE NIGHT

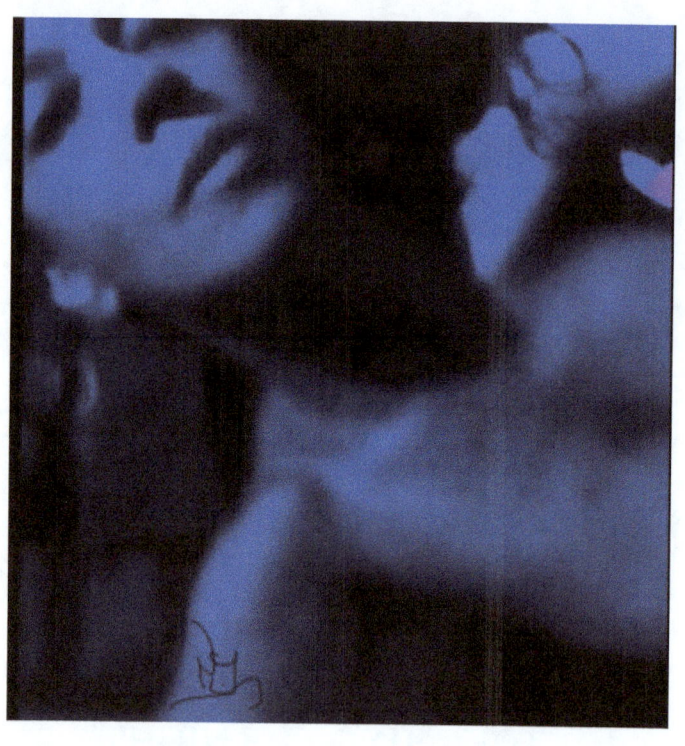

The year of 2021 I entered into
the sixtieth decade of my life in this
wonderful planet Earth.

I feel the need to acknowledge
all the unique teachers
I've encountered during my

life journey, starting with my parents,
nephews, family, friends, cousins,
aunties, brothers and sisters either by
blood or by soul or by nature,
fashion creators, those aggregates
animals and/or humans which also
include amazing extraordinary
gurus, artists, bodhisattvas,

musicians, visual artists, tutors, art directors, fairies, witches, magicians, actors and actresses, tour guides, gnomes, alchemists, relatives and relatives-by-law, school teachers and private ones, as well as all
my students – past, present, future, some bank managers,
hotels, airlines, stores representatives, drivers, neighbours, consumerism centres,
social medias network,
public offices, and so many other companies representatives, etc, for their love and compassion towards my double Aries Leo Moon

way of learning to best

behave within the collectiveness, by

the sharing of some other glimpses

in the form of an illustrative insight-

ful bonus in the form of poetic im-

ages,

poetic reflections, poetic lines for you

my reader, now, that are here still

beautifully accompanying

this wording flow of mine

to whom

I dearly thank from

the bottom of my heart

... >   If   < ...

if

there is an

opening to

the belief in the

possibility

of breaking bonds

once parts can be accepted

as a completeness in itself

that makes

it easier

to cope

with ideas and practicing

of separation

by breaking a bond it shall mean a

way beyond

the destruction of a previous

structure

by breaking

a bond

it shall signalise

the reestablishment of

the original

bond-free

state of mind

... >   so   < ...

the world might be taken for

a reversed

fixed

whole format

commitments might begin

to

be re...

...establis'd

...taken

by

parts

into

parts

parts that seem

to be

like...

...the image

of

ourselves...

...images

of

ourselves...

...at these

contemporary

days...

SHADES

Shapes

The parts

and

The whole

What are we-what we do-what we think-what we get-?

What is the role of art in our days?

Who cares for the arts?

Who pays?

Who receives?

What means to profit from arts?

Where can arts lead us all?

Shall arts live forever?

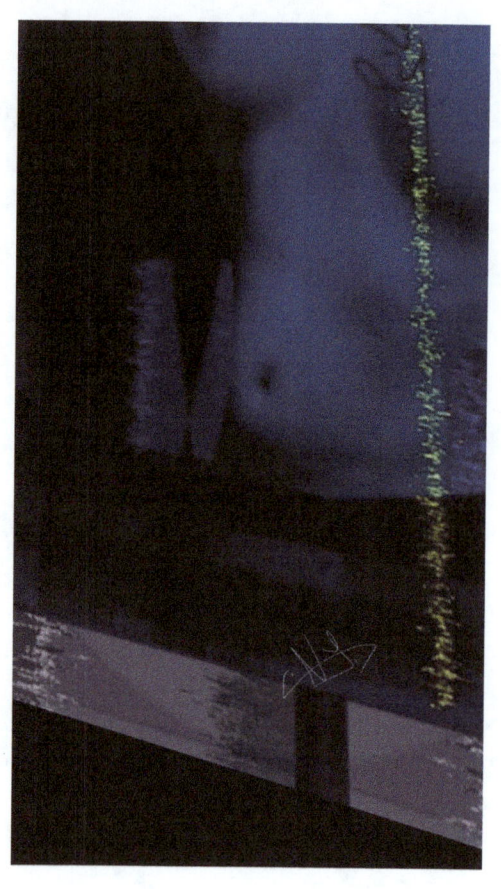

How far can we preserve the arts
from disappearing from humanity?

Can humanity make sense without
any artistic perspective?

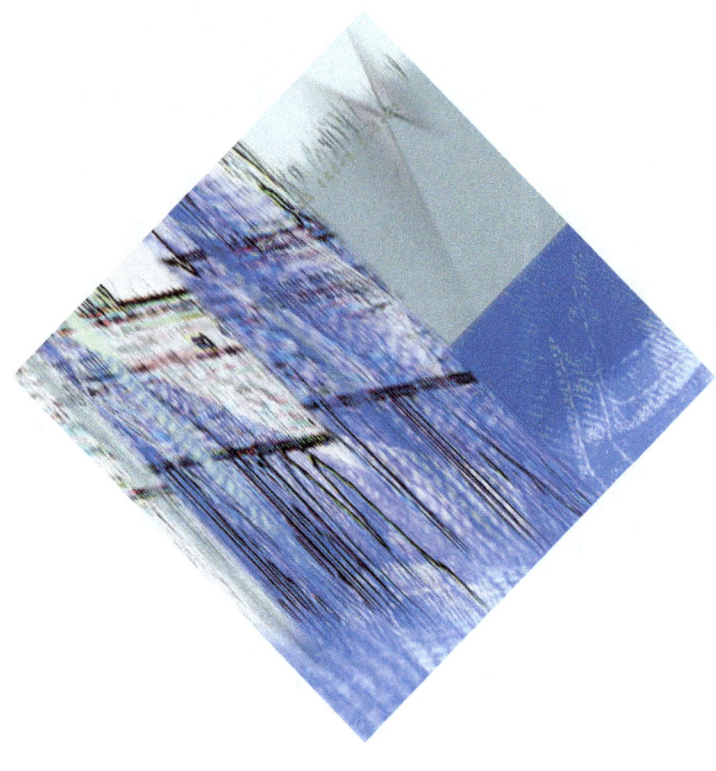

Virtual Design Composition on Jeans Pants
photography & design by Silvia Prado dos Anjos
(nylaia prado dos anjos)

... so ...

which sign shall
I follow
for
life's road
no maps
to guide

honking dots
knots
ranger
to rendering ev'o'ultionary
revoluti on
c oo perate
on n'neess
om
aum
on
so b on g
so
bunk
so dance
so
smiling

glimpses
all a long

... >   < ...

I walk
I talk
I search
'n call
rain touches
my skin
what shall I do

I watch my steps
drip drops splashes
rolling along

to disappear down
by the walkway

I walk
I talk
I search
'n call
rain touches
my skin
what shall I do

my feet
print
water dreams

door

'n

site

the dance

of

matter

I walk

I talk

I search

'n call

I touch

my skin

what can be

still

whatsoever
whatsoever

for tomorrow

now

sleeps

I come to sit
by the
front door
of the
house

by myself
by myself
by myself

...

so

...

I talk
I walk
I search
'n call
blues touch
my skin

what
can
be still

glimpses of
last night

out of
my senses

whatsoever
whatsoever

I have traveled
in time and space

what do I fear

the truth of
this new
born light
to guide
into eternal risk

man
woman
to be forever
the greatest
challenge
of
that

all

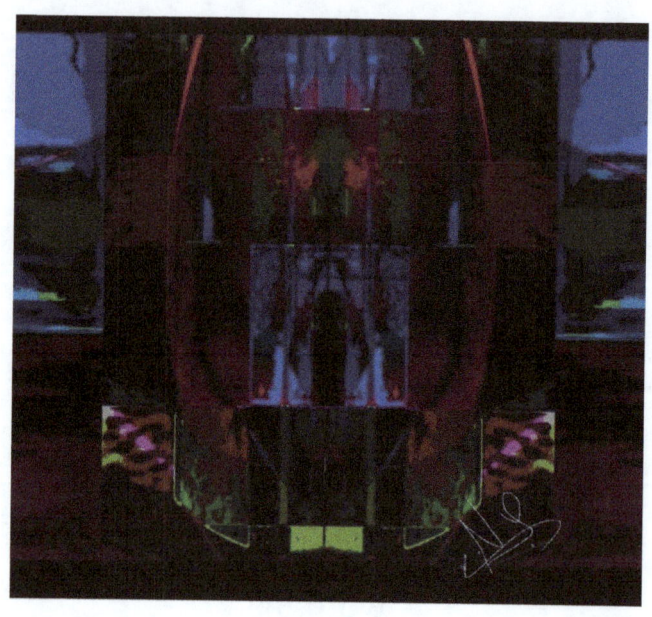

that
all the ways
pushes

the beaming
of
stars

whatsoever
whatsoever

the beaming
ofstars

life bits
biting memories
beckon
to

unbreath'd
unset
blue frozen
gaps

like éclairs

like cozy arms
around waits

like wings
braving atmospherical
push 'n pull

what's up

what's lacking

... by accepting
the
risk
of
happiness

to
embracing

to recycling
life's
opening

to
embracing
the feel
of
the
rising
afar from
gravity

whatsoever

I talk
I walk
I search

I
am
all
I touch
my skin
I sing
to
the
beaming
of
blue
stars

whatsoever

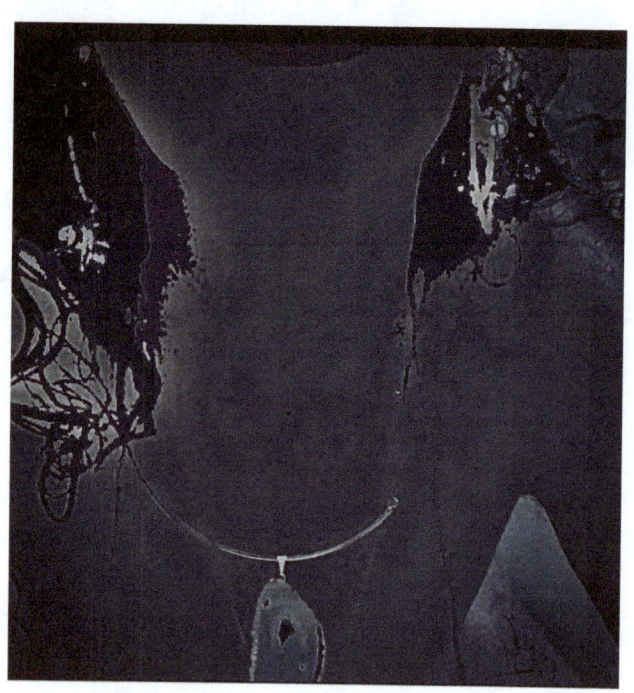

www.ingramcontent.com/pod-product-compliance
Lightning Source LLC
Chambersburg PA
CBHW070121230526
45472CB00004B/1362